THE MYSTERIOUS CAMARILLA EQUATION

TRADER'S HOLY GRAIL DECODED

José Manuel Moreira Batista

"Books like these- I consider hidden gems. Not many people know about it, but it definitely is a fantastic read. I admire how knowledgeable the author is in writing this book. He answers a ton of questions that I've had for a long, long time regarding the Camarilla Equation- it's as if he was reading my mind. I highly recommend it for you traders out there!" - *JP*

"Excellent book. Straight to the point and clear. Contains all the information needed to use the Camarilla Equation. " - *Martinez*

"I will recommend this book to all my colleagues." - *Prosper T.*

"I really loved this book... It kept me thinking and my brain working all the way through it.... I love books that have to do with numbers and I love giving my brain a good challenge..... The book is very well written and is very interesting with lots of facts that I never knew about... I love how it's broken down and made so anyone can understand and that you don't have to be a math genius to read it... Looking forward to reading more great books from the author..." - *Amazon Customer 360*

"Finally a readable book about the camarilla pivot points. Also includes testing tools. For serious traders." - *Leonel Trachu*

INTRODUCTION

ARTHUR: If you will not show us the Grail, we shall take your castle by force!

GUARD: You don't frighten us, English pig-dogs! Go and boil your bottoms, sons of a silly person. I blow my nose at you, so-called Arthur-king, you and all your silly English kaniggets. Thppppt!

GALAHAD: What a strange person.

ARTHUR: Now look here, my good man!

GUARD: I don't want to talk to you no more, you empty headed animal food trough water! I fart in your general direction! You mother was a hamster and your father smelt of elderberries!

GALAHAD: Is there someone else up there we could talk to?

GUARD: No, now go away or I shall taunt you a second time-a!

~ Monty Python and the Holy Grail

The Mysterious Camarilla Equation: Trader's Holy Grail Decoded is a glimpse behind the curtain of this supposedly widely popular and extremely effective trading system that paradoxically remains mostly unexplored. It gives the reader a working knowledge of the Camarilla Equation as well as the tools to analyze it further.

The Mysterious Camarilla Equation: Trader's Holy Grail Decoded starts with a birds-eye view of the curious origins of the *camarilla* and then proceeds to review its formulas and trading guidelines.

A testing procedure is laid out to assess the trading performance of the Camarilla Equation. Readers can freely download a testing tool using the link inside the book.

Trade with common sense, have fun and make profits!

José Manuel Moreira Batista

Table of Contents

A mysterious name

The first mysterious element of the Camarilla Equation is its name. Somehow *camarilla* is a word that immediately conveys the feeling that we are facing something obscure and enigmatic. It is a Spanish word, defined in the *Diccionario de la Real Academia Española*, the reference dictionary for the Spanish language, as "A group of persons who surreptitiously influence state or other higher authority decisions." *Wikipedia* and *Merriam Webster* concur, highlighting that this lobbying is carried by "unofficial advisors" in a "behind-the-scenes process". The term appears to have been used for the first time during Ferdinand VII's second reign in Spain, from 1813 to 1833. His autocratic regimen was directed by a camarilla of his favorites. The word favorite referred to persons of both sexes who had various degrees of intimacy and influence with a monarch or his spouse.

The most notorious camarillas were to be found later in Germany, with the word Kamarilla making its way into the German vocabulary. Prince Philipp zu Eulenburg was reputedly the head of what came to be known as Kaiser's Willhelm II of Germany Gay Camarilla. He was repeatedly attacked in the newspaper Die Zukunft by Maximilian Harden, its Jewish anti-monarchist publisher. Harden denounced Eulenberg as "the leader of a sinister and effeminate camarilla" that also included the military commander of Berlin Count Kuno von Moltke. Homosexuality was then a criminal offense and the biggest scandal of the second German Reich ensued. Eulenberg and other prominent figures were eventually put on trial but nothing much came from it. In spite of his tribulations Eulenberg's influence continued through the many friends he had in government and in the military. He was a strong supporter of German expansionism before and during First World War. After the war he apparently reconsidered his bellicose views. He died in 1921, one year before Maximilian Harden was severely beaten by members of the Freikorps, (paramilitary nationalist organizations with a strong anti-communist bend). Sturmabteilung (S.A.) leader Ernst Röhm, Schutzstaffel (S.S.) leader Heinrich Himmler, and Reich Protector of Bohemia and Moravia Reinhard Heydrich, among many others who later became Nazi leaders, were members of the Freikorps.

Elected the second President of the Second Reich, German war hero Field Marshall Paul von Hindenburg also surrounded himself with a camarilla. It was led by his own son, Oskar von Hindenburg, and included Otto Meissner, General Wilhelm Groener, and General Kurt von Schleicher. Curiously, this camarilla drew its power from... - a formula! It was known as the 25/48/53 Formula, the numbers alluding to the three articles in the Weimar's Republic Constitution that allowed for the formation of a presidential government. Years of scheming and political maneuvering, in particular by Schleicher, ended by facilitating the ascent of Adolph Hitler to the Chancellor in January 1933.

After Hindenburg's death in the following year, the presidency was suspended, the Reichstag dissolved and all the power in Germany was concentrated in the hands of Hitler and his own Nazi camarilla. Schleicher was one of those gunned down in his house on June 30, 1934 during the bloody episode known as the Night of the Long Knives.

The Nazi regime and some of its key figures have often been linked to occultism and mysticism, obscure secret societies, conspiracy theories and even vampire tales. The widely popular Masquerade books identify a large sect of vampires who aims to fit in among humans so as to more easily feed on them. Its name: The Camarilla.

As the end of the Second World War neared, there was a massive recruitment of German scientists by the U.S.A., the most visible and widely known part of which culminated in The Manhattan Project and the development of the atomic bomb. However, the scope and extent of the American brain snatching effort is only now slowly coming to light. *The Paperclip Conspiracy: The Hunt for the Nazi Scientists* by Tom Bower and *Hitler's Suppressed and Still-Secret Weapons* by Henry Stevens are two of the ever growing number of works that attempt to shed light on what really happened.

Unquestionably, Nazi Germany had the most advanced scientific and technological knowledge of the world in a wide range of areas. U.S.A. was the main beneficiary of that intellectual output. Conceivably U.S.S.R. (now Russia) and the United Kingdom benefited as well, albeit on a much smaller scale. Some of the records have probably been lost, destroyed or hidden. In other cases they were surreptitiously sold, as happened in West Berlin in February 1988. On that occasion, tens of thousands of Nazi files disappeared from a records office, presumably acquired by military dealers and memorabilia collectors.

A mysterious trader

Internet lore has it that in 1989, a few months after the Nazi documents vanished, as conspiracy theorists would point out, "a successful bond trader named Nick Scott discovered the Camarilla Equation while day trading".

Who was Nick Scott? An Internet search for "Nick Scott" turns out a few individuals who obviously cannot be the man in question. A number of sites repeat the story that he is the brains behind the equation without adding any other relevant information or questioning the fact. The only seemingly bright spot is the site **CamarillaEquation.com** that transcribes an interview with the elusive trader.

CamarillaEquation.com is a peculiar site in that it has no "About Us" or "Contact Us" pages. Most of its information relates to day trading with the Camarilla Equation and dates back to 2003, the year the domain was registered. The site seems to serve basically as a placeholder for the Nick Scott interview and pointer to another site, **SureFireThing.com** (more about it later).

In this famous interview, Nick Scott is described as a tall, overweight middle-aged man who has a fancy for hitting the bottle but possesses a sharp intellect. The conversation is said to take place in a bar located in the upscale neighborhood where Scott lives with his wife and children. The text has no photos of either the locale, the interviewee or the interviewer, whose identity is never mentioned.

There are two themes in the short interview. The first tries to establish Nick Scott as an intellectual heavyweight with "a classical education at a top flight school" and a superior trader: "The reason I'm Nick Scott and you are not is that I adapt on a daily basis." The interview also hints at the broad sources of inspiration for the equation: pattern recognition, Fibonacci numbers, Steidlmayer's Market Profile, and even an erroneous reference to the Golden Mean (an Aristotelian philosophical concept), confusing it with the Golden Ratio (a mathematical relationship between two numbers).

If one wanted to establish someone's credentials as a big shot financial market operator in the roaring '80s the "bond trader" label would certainly go a long way in helping achieve that objective. As Federal Reserve chairman Paul Volcker tightened the money supply to combat inflation, interest rates rose to record levels and so did bond trading. Widening federal budget deficits added fire to the fixed-income arena as Treasury securities supply ballooned. The Savings and Loans industry joined the speculative frenzy after being deregulated by Congress. Michael Milken came up with the revolutionary junk bond concept, which fueled the take-over fever that promptly ensued. Legions of university business graduates still wet behind the ears were minted into investment bankers and made millions overnight advising on the decade mega-deals. In Tom Wolfe's 1897 best-seller The Bonfire of the Vanities, the central character was "master of the universe" bond trader Sherman McCoy. Two years later Michael Lewis' Liar's Poker hit the shelves, recounting his experiences as a bond salesman in Salomon's Brothers. Successful bond trader Nick Scott surely rubbed elbows with the right crowd!

The second theme of the interview takes us to the third mystery, which is the equation itself.

A mysterious tale

A *Google* search for "Camarilla Equation" returns close to 48,000 results. Several of the results spell out *a* Camarilla Equation. Some of the sites where one can find the equation state they have "found it", "discovered it" or "figured it out". Some attribute its origin to "successful bond trader Nick Scott", while others say they have "found it on the Web." There are also those who do not say anything at all about its provenance.

So are there dozens of different equations out there? No. The various versions of the equation turn out to be pretty consistent, that is to say, they have basically the same formulation with minor variations. To put it in a different way, they probably have the same root. This means that either they were copied from the same source, or several people reverse engineered it and arrived at the same set of original formulas, or both.

That takes us back to the second theme of the interview, a series of snippets aimed at distinguishing the original and secret Camarilla Equation from copycat versions available on the Internet. According to it, the true Camarilla Equation has never been revealed and Nick Scott licenses it only through the **SureFireThing.com** site. The equation entails a "very convoluted process" which "won't fit in a few lines of code". Nick Scott emphasizes that the complexity of the math involved makes it very unlikely that other people have found the equation. In his words, other versions of the Camarilla Equation "don't work as well as the real deal, I'm told."

A visit to the **SureFireThing.com** site reveals it also lacks the "About Us" page. It does have a "Contact Us" section although one has to register first to be able to use it. This is a membership site, buying the monthly subscription ($179 the last time I checked) allows access to the SureFireThing's Camarilla Equation, the one and only developed by the successful bond trader Nick Scott. This is also the only site found in the *Google* search that actually charges for the equation, all the others share it freely.

Speculations

What is to be made of all of this? Are Nick Scott and the interview nothing but a fabrication? With the available evidence, that certainly cannot be ruled out. But why would anyone go to all that trouble? There are several possible answers, all stemming from the willingness to make money selling the equation instead of simply trading with it. For that, all one needs is a broker.

Speculation 1

Suppose John Doe stumbles upon the equation and wants to sell it. Being John Doe he does not have any particular credibility to help him market the system. But John is a creative guy and he comes up with a fancy mysterious name, the Camarilla Equation. To add credibility, he spins the tale of it being developed by a super bond trader, Nick Scott. Sales start rolling in and the future seems bright. Then some of the traders who have been using the equation figure it out and begin sharing it. Sales plummet. What to do? Again, John Doe comes up with a brilliant idea: to interview Nick Scott and differentiate the original, true and secret equation from all those damned copycats!

Speculation 2

Another possibility: suppose the developer of the equation is the real deal. He truly is a well-known "trader extraordinaire." He wants to sell his invention but his divorcing wife is taking him to the cleaners, or his working contract forces him to surrender any intellectual property to his employer, or for whatever other reason he does not want his real name to be associated with this venture. What should he do? Hmm... - How about a slight change of name?

Speculation 3

Third scenario: Trader Tim bought a document with mathematical formulas that, upon experimentation, become the basis of a rather promising trading system. Unfortunately, the author of the document, although a brilliant mind, has a dark past and is strongly associated with some unsavory characters. Tim realizes he needs an alternate story to package and market the system.

It is often said that reality is stranger than fiction but whatever the truth is about the origins of the Camarilla Equation and the real identity of its developer, the real important question to be answered is: -*Does it work?*

A brief review

Fundamental concepts

The Camarilla Equation is based on technical analysis which aims to forecast future prices by assessing the balance of power between the forces of supply and demand. Technical analysis has as its basic tenets, that:

a) The market discounts everything;

b) The price moves in trends;

c) History repeats itself.

It is worth briefly reviewing the technical analysis tools that appear to more closely relate to the Camarilla Equation formulation and its trade positioning. The main concepts that allow for the testing of a trading strategy are concisely described in this section.

Price

At any given moment the price of an asset represents the consensus expectations of the buyers (who expect the price to go higher) and the sellers (who expect the price to go lower). Several types of prices are often used:

Open - the price for the first trade of the period (e.g., the very first trade in the morning).

High - the highest price that was traded during the period. At this point more sellers than buyers started to show up.

Low - the lowest price that was traded during the period. At this point more buyers than sellers started to show up.

Close - the price for the last trade of the period (e.g., the very last trade in the afternoon).

Median - the average of the high and the low prices for the period.

Typical - the average of the high, the low and the close prices for the period.

Weighted close - the sum of the high, the low and twice the close price divided by four.

(Price) Range - the difference between the highest and the lowest price.

For example, on April 21 the S&P 500 index opened at 1,865.79 hit a high of 1,871.89 and a low of 1,863.18 and closed at 1,871.89. The calculated values are:

Median: (1,871.89 + 1,863.18) / 2 = 1,867.54

Typical: $(1{,}871.89 + 1{,}863.18 + 1{,}871.89) / 3 = 1{,}868.99$

Weighted close: $(1{,}871.89 + 1{,}863.18 + 1{,}871.89 \times 2) / 4 = 1{,}869.71$

Range: $1{,}871.89 - 1{,}863.18 = 8.71.$

Trends

A trend is the general direction of the price. There are uptrends (the price is moving higher) and downtrends (the price is moving lower) and sideways movement (absence of a clear uptrend or downtrend).

An **uptrend** is formed by a series of higher highs and higher lows. An upward trendline is a line drawn at the lows of an upward trend.

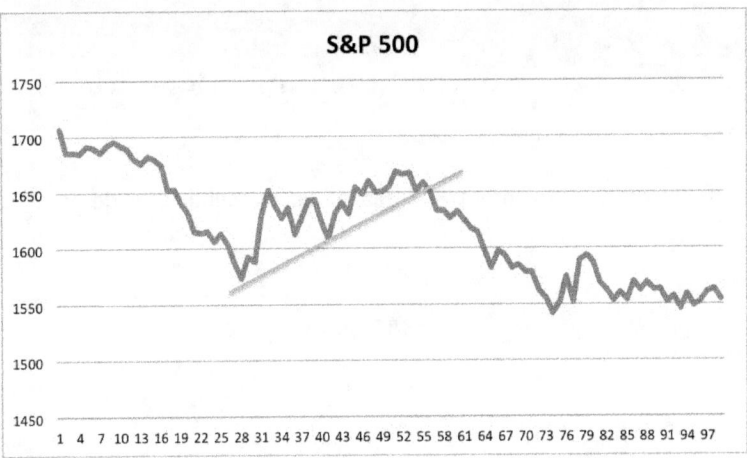

Uptrend in an S&P 500 index chart.

A **downtrend** is formed by a series of lower lows and lower highs. A downward trendline is a line drawn at the highs of the downward trend.

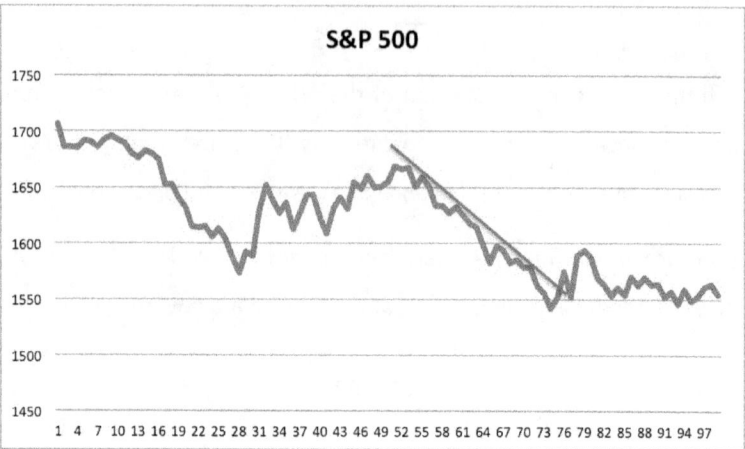

Downtrend in an S&P 500 index chart.

A **sideways** or horizontal trend has no clear ascending or descending action.

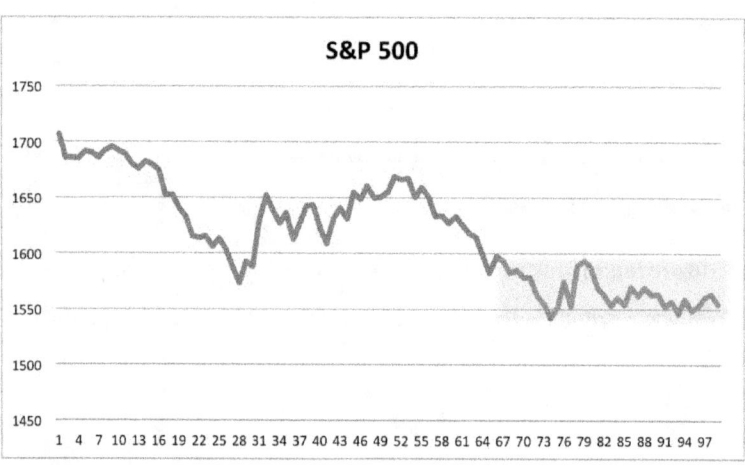

Sideways in an S&P 500 index chart.

Support and resistance

Support is the price level below which the market participants do not expect the asset price to fall. Conversely **resistance** is the price level above which the market participants do not expect the asset price to climb. At support a lot of buyers are willing to buy the asset. At resistance a lot of sellers are willing to sell it. If a support or resistance level is broken that means the expectations have changed. Often if the price falls below a support level, that level will then become resistance. Conversely if the price rises above a resistance level, it will become support.

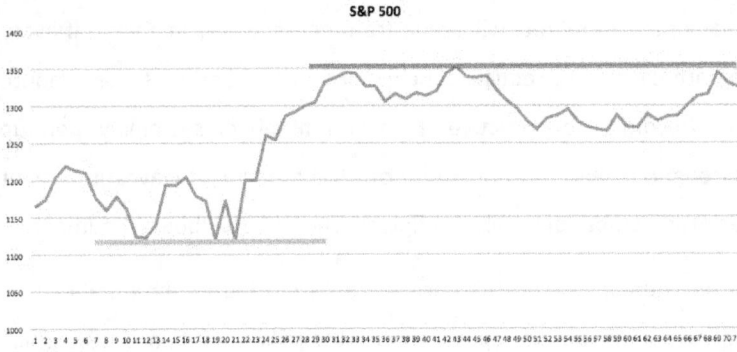

Support (green) and Resistance (red).

Fibonacci numbers

Leonardo Pisano Bigollo, known as Fibonacci, was a very important Italian mathematician of the 13th century, who introduced the Hindu–Arabic numeral system in Europe. He also spread the word about a sequence of numbers that came to be known as the Fibonacci numbers. In a Fibonacci sequence, the first two numbers are by definition 0 and 1 and afterwards each number in the series is the sum of the previous two numbers:

0, 1, 1, 2, 3, 5, 8, 13, 21, 34, 55, 89, 144, etc.

It seems this sequence was developed to answer the question of how many pairs of rabbits will result from one first pair in a year, if every month each pair produces a new pair which, from the second month on, becomes reproductive. Fibonacci numbers seemingly pop up throughout the natural world. Both the number of leaves in a plant and the number of petals in a flower tend to be a Fibonacci number.

If one number in the Fibonacci series is divided by the number that follows it, one obtains approximately the **golden ratio**, or 61.8% which is found in several natural proportions. Other significant ratios are obtained by dividing one number in the series by the one that is placed 2, 3, etc., places to the right. For instance: 89/144 = 61.8%, 55/144 = 38.2%, 34/144 = 23.6%.

Fibonacci numbers and ratios

Series	Ratio N / N+1	Ratio N / N+2	Ratio N / N+3
1	0.500	0.333	0.200
2	0.667	0.400	0.250
3	0.600	0.375	0.231
5	0.625	0.385	0.238
8	0.615	0.381	0.235
13	0.619	0.382	0.236
21	0.618	0.382	0.236
34	0.618	0.382	0.236
55	0.618	0.382	0.236
89	0.618	0.382	0.236
144	0.618	0.382	0.236
233	0.618	0.382	0.236
377	0.618	0.382	0.236

Fibonacci numbers

For mysterious reasons, these ratios determine important levels of support and resistance for asset prices. The levels are calculated using a process known as **Fibonacci retracements**. This consists of taking one high and one low point in a chart and dividing the chart by the

Fibonacci ratios. The levels identified by this process are support and resistance levels.

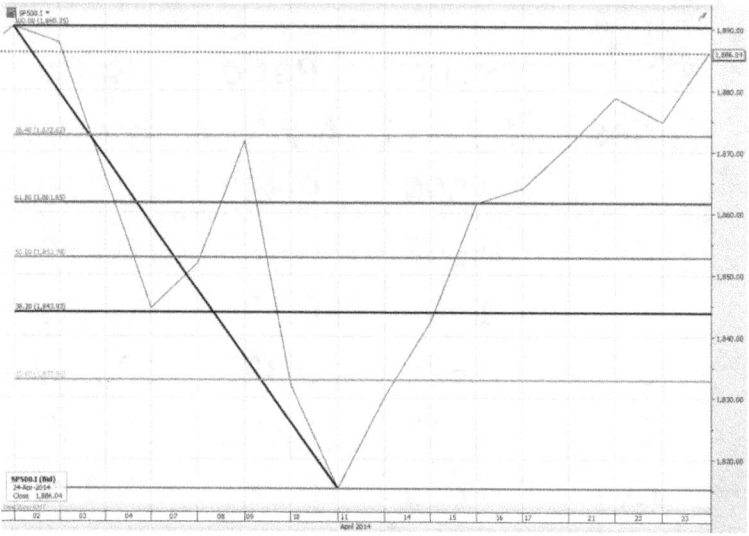

Fibonacci retracement - *Chart from Saxo Bank's SaxoTrader2 platform.*

On April 2 the S&P500 closed at 1,890.35. In the following days it fell and on April 11 it closed at 1,815.23. Taking these two points as high and low, the chart above shows the Fibonacci retracement levels. On April 23, the S&P500 closed at 1,875.39 on its way back to the previous 1,890.35 having surpassed key resistance levels.

Mean reversion

The tendency of prices to converge (regress) on an average value over time is called **mean reversion**. For instance, if the recent price of a stock significantly exceeds its long-term average, it can be expected to fall in the near future as it reverts to its mean. Likewise, if the recent price of a stock has been significantly below its long-term average, it can be expected to rise in the near future.

There might be fundamental reasons that justify the departure from an historic mean (for example, think of the iPod introduction by Apple). Mean reversion works often but there is a point where it simply stops working.

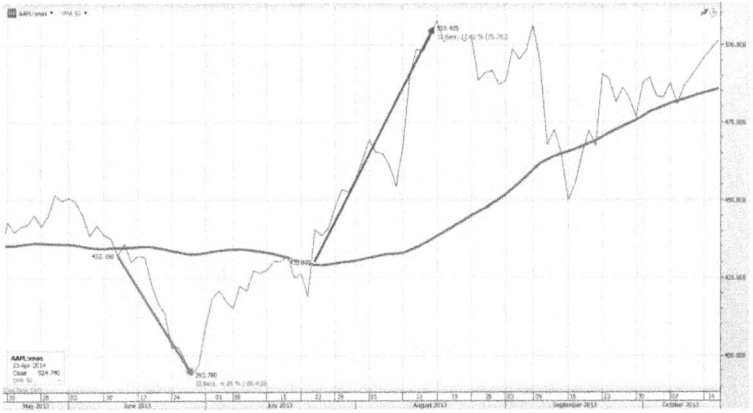

Mean reversion (AAPL) - *Chart from Saxo Bank's SaxoTrader2 platform.*

Breakouts

When the price of an asset moves through either support or resistance a **breakout** occurs. Sometimes the term breakout is used to refer to a move through resistance and the term *breakdown* is used to refer to a move through support.

When a **breakout** occurs, more buying is likely to come and a further increase in price can be expected. The previous resistance level now becomes a **support** level.

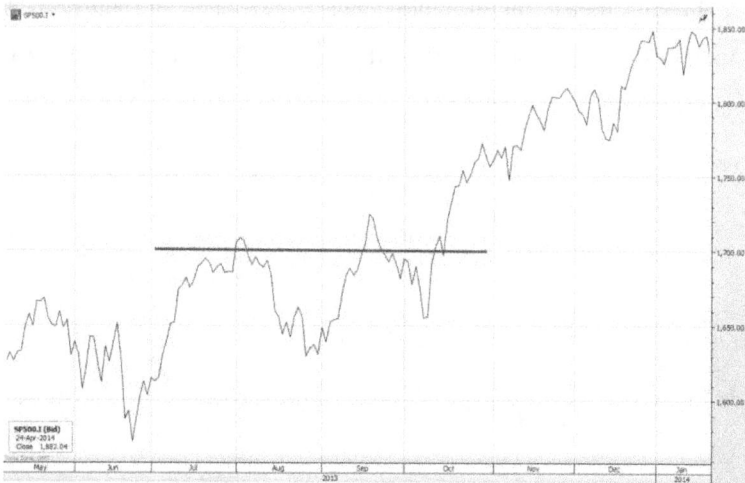

Breakout - *Chart from Saxo Bank's SaxoTrader2 platform.*

When a **breakdown** occurs, more selling is likely to come and a further decrease in price can be expected. The previous support level now becomes a resistance level.

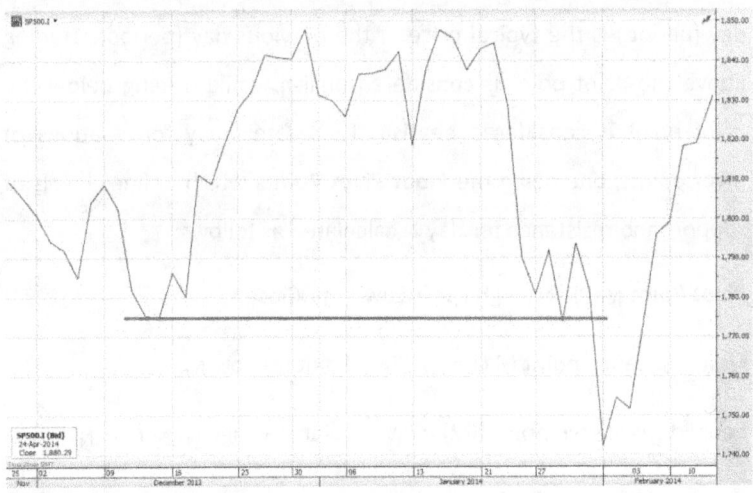

Breakdown - *Chart from Saxo Bank's SaxoTrader2 platform.*

Pivot points

These are technical analysis indicators used to determine the overall trend of the market over different time frames. The pivot point for a day (period) is the typical price of the previous day (period). Trading above the pivot point is considered bullish, while trading below the pivot point is considered bearish. There are many formulations of pivot points, one being the **Floor Pivot Points** which defines levels of support and resistance for day N calculated as follows:

Pivot Point $_N$ (PP) = (High $_{N-1}$ + Low $_{N-1}$ + Close $_{N-1}$) / 3

First resistance point (R1) = 2 x Pivot Point $_N$ - Low $_{N-1}$

Second resistance point (R2) = Pivot Point $_N$ + High $_{N-1}$ - Low $_{N-1}$

Third resistance point (R3) = High $_{N-1}$ + 2 x (Pivot Point $_N$ - Low $_{N-1}$)

First support point (S1) = 2 x Pivot Point $_N$ - High $_{N-1}$

Second support point (S2) = Pivot Point $_N$ - High $_{N-1}$ + Low $_{N-1}$

Third support point (S3) = Low $_{N-1}$ - 2 x (High $_{N-1}$ - Pivot Point $_N$)

Recall that on April 21 the S&P 500 index had a high of 1,871.89, a low of 1,863.18 and closed at 1,871.89. For April 22, the floor pivot points calculations are:

PP = (1,871.89 + 1,863.18 + 1,871. 89) / 3 = 1,868.99

R1 = 2 x 1,868.99 − 1,863.18 = 1,874.79

R2 = 1,868.99 + 1,871.89 - 1,863.18 = 1,877.70

R3 = 1,871.89 + 2 x (1,868.99 - 1,863.18) = 1,883.50

S1 = 2 x 1,868.99 – 1,871.89 = 1,866.08

S2 = 1,868.99 – 1,871.89 + 1,863.18 = 1,860.28

S3 = 1,863.18 - 2 x (1,871.89 – 1,868.99) = 1,857.37

Win and loss ratios

The **win ratio** of a trading strategy is obtained by dividing the number of successful trades it generated by the total number of trades it generated:

Win ratio = Number of winning trades / total number of trades

The **loss ratio** is calculated by deducting the win ratio from 1:

Loss ratio = 1 - (win ratio)

Reward to risk

The **reward to risk ratio** is a comparison between the average amount earned when a trading strategy makes a successful trade and the average amount lost when it makes an unsuccessful trade:

Reward to risk ratio = (average win amount if trade is successful) / (average loss amount if trade is unsuccessful)

The **limit reward to risk ratio** is a comparison between the maximum amount earned when a trading strategy makes a successful trade and the maximum amount lost when it makes an unsuccessful trade:

Limit reward to risk ratio = (maximum win amount if trade is successful) / (maximum loss amount if trade is unsuccessful).

Expectancy

The **expectancy** of a trading strategy is a measure that combines the reward to risk ratio and the win and loss ratios and tells us if the strategy is profitable in the long run.

Expectancy = (reward to risk) x (win ratio) - (loss ratio)

If a strategy has a positive expectancy then it will earn money in the long run. If the trade's expectancy is negative, it will lose money and should not be traded. If Strategy A has a higher expectancy than Strategy B, then we should prefer Strategy A to Strategy B.

The **limit expectancy** is calculated the same way but using the limit reward to risk instead of the normal (average) reward to risk.

The Camarilla Equation

The 6x6 equation

As previously mentioned, there are several versions of the Camarilla Equation available on sites and forums all over the Internet. I am going to present the seemingly more comprehensive formulation that calculates six support and six resistance levels, whereas most other versions calculate only four.

The Camarilla' Equation starts by calculating the previous period price range (highest price - lowest price). It proceeds to increase that range by 10% and then successively adds one twelfth, one sixth, one fourth and one half of that value to the previous period close price to determine the first four resistance levels. The first four support levels are set symmetrically, subtracting the same values from the previous period close price.

The last two resistance and support levels are calculated building on the previous four levels as described ahead, and with a little help from the famous 1.168 Fibonacci number.

Resistance levels

The **resistance levels** are calculated as follows:

Resistance level 1 (R1) = Close $_{N-1}$ + Range $_{N-1}$ x 1.1 / 12

Resistance level 2 (R2) = Close $_{N-1}$ + Range $_{N-1}$ x 1.1 / 6

Resistance level 3 (R3) = Close $_{N-1}$ + Range $_{N-1}$ x 1.1 / 4

Resistance level 4 (R4) = Close $_{N-1}$ + Range $_{N-1}$ x 1.1 / 2

Resistance level 5 (R5) = R4 + (R4 - R3) x 1.168

Resistance level 6 (R6) = High $_{N-1}$ / Low $_{N-1}$ x Close $_{N-1}$

The calculation for the first four resistance levels always follow the same pattern: it simply adds a growing fraction of the previous day range increased by 10% to the previous day closing price. The fifth resistance is obtained by adding to R4 a Fibonacci multiple of the difference between R4 and R3. Finally, one gets to the sixth resistance level by applying the previous day price variation to the previous day closing price.

For April 22 the resistance points are therefore:

R1= 1,871.89 + 8,71 x 1.1 / 12 = 1,872.69

R2 = 1,871.89 + 8,71 x 1.1 / 6 = 1,873.49

R3 = 1,871.89 + 8,71 x 1.1 / 4 = 1,874.29

R4 = 1,871.89 + 8,71 x 1.1 / 2 = 1,876.68

R5 = 1,876.68 + (1,876.68 − 1,874.28) x 1.168 = 1,879.48

R6 = 1,871.89 / 1,863.18 x 1,871.89 = 1,880.64

Support levels

The **support levels** are calculated as follows:

Support level 1 (S1) = Close $_{N-1}$ - Range $_{N-1}$ x 1.1 / 12

Support level 2 (S2) = Close $_{N-1}$ - Range $_{N-1}$ x 1.1 / 6

Support level 3 (S3) = Close $_{N-1}$ - Range $_{N-1}$ x 1.1 / 4

Support level 4 (S4) = Close $_{N-1}$ - Range $_{N-1}$ x 1.1 / 2

Support level 5 (S5) = S4 - (S3 - S4) x 1.168

Support level 6 (S6) = Close $_{N-1}$ - (R6 - Close $_{N-1}$)

The calculation of the first four support levels always follow the same pattern: it simply subtracts from the previous day closing price a growing fraction of the previous day range increased by 10%. The fifth support is obtained by subtracting from S4 a Fibonacci multiple of the difference between S3 and S4. Finally, one gets to the sixth support level by subtracting from the previous day closing price its difference to R6.

For April 22 the support levels are therefore:

S1 = 1,871.89 – 8.71 x 1.1 / 12 = 1,871.09

S2 = 1,871.89 – 8.71 x 1.1 / 6 = 1,870.29

S3 = 1,871.89 – 8.71 x 1.1 / 4 = 1,869.49

S4 = 1,871.89 – 8.71 x 1.1 / 2 = 1,867.11

S5 = 1,867.11 - (1,869.49 – 1,867.11) x 1.168 = 1,864.30

S6 = 1,871.89 - (1,880.64 – 1,871.89) = 1,863.14.

Trading guidelines

The Camarilla Equation gives specific trading recommendations based on the position of the opening price relative to its calculated resistance and support levels. In addition, unlike most trading systems that are either mean reversion or trend following oriented, the Camarilla Equation suggests both reversal and breakout trades.

Reversal trades

If the open price falls in the interval between the support level 3 (S3) and the resistance level 3 (R3), a mean reversal trade is on the horizon.

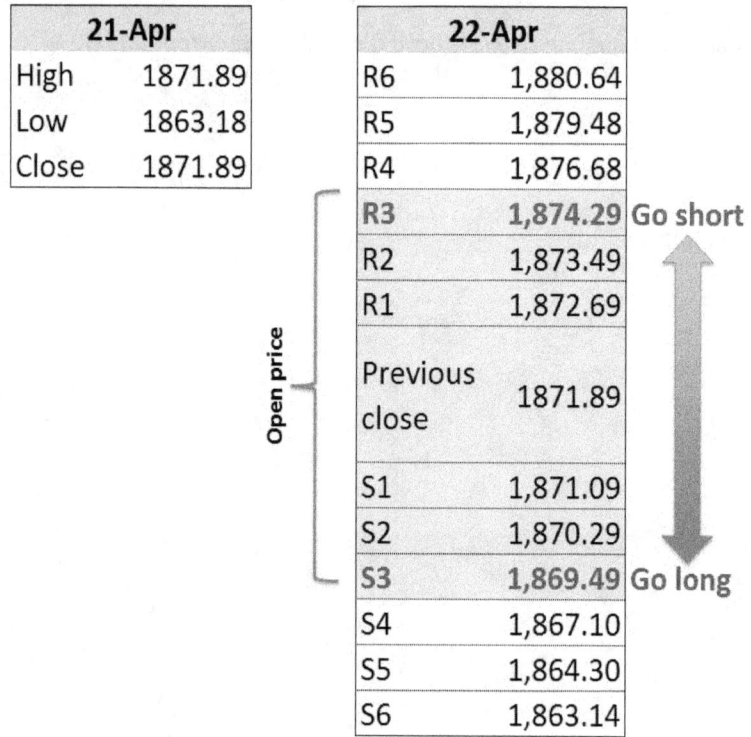

21-Apr	
High	1871.89
Low	1863.18
Close	1871.89

22-Apr		
R6	1,880.64	
R5	1,879.48	
R4	1,876.68	
R3	1,874.29	Go short
R2	1,873.49	
R1	1,872.69	
Previous close	1871.89	
S1	1,871.09	
S2	1,870.29	
S3	1,869.49	Go long
S4	1,867.10	
S5	1,864.30	
S6	1,863.14	

Reversal trade entering range

A. *Go long* when price hits S3. Profit targets are R1, R2 and R3 and stop loss is S4.

22-Apr		
R6	1,880.64	
R5	1,879.48	
R4	1,876.68	
R3	1,874.29	
R2	1,873.49	Profit targets
R1	1,872.69	
Previous close	1871.89	
S1	1,871.09	
S2	1,870.29	
S3	1,869.49	Go long
S4	1,867.10	Stop loss
S5	1,864.30	
S6	1,863.14	

Long reversal trade

B. Go short when price hits R3. Profit targets are S1, S2 and S3 and stop loss is R4.

22-Apr		
R6	1,880.64	
R5	1,879.48	
R4	1,876.68	Stop loss
R3	1,874.29	Go short
R2	1,873.49	
R1	1,872.69	
Previous close	1871.89	
S1	1,871.09	
S2	1,870.29	Profit targets
S3	1,869.49	
S4	1,867.10	
S5	1,864.30	
S6	1,863.14	

Short reversal trade

Breakout trades

If the open price falls in the interval between resistance level 3 (R3) and resistance level 4 (R4) or between support level 3 (S3) and support level 3 (S4), a breakout trade is on the horizon.

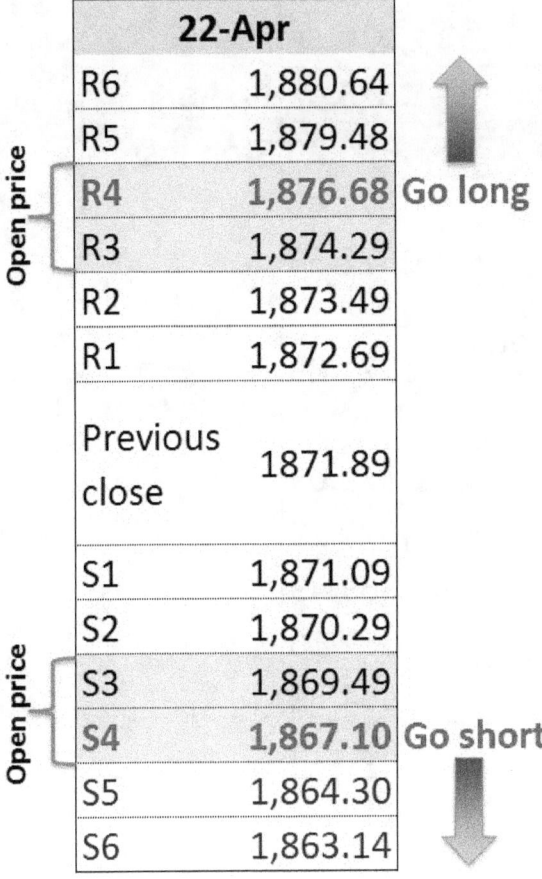

22-Apr	
R6	1,880.64
R5	1,879.48
R4	1,876.68 Go long
R3	1,874.29
R2	1,873.49
R1	1,872.69
Previous close	1871.89
S1	1,871.09
S2	1,870.29
S3	1,869.49
S4	1,867.10 Go short
S5	1,864.30
S6	1,863.14

Breakout trade entering range.

A. Go long when price hits R4. Profit targets are R5 and R6. Stop loss is R3.

22-Apr	
R6	1,880.64	Profit
R5	1,879.48	targets
R4	1,876.68	Go long
R3	1,874.29	Stop loss
R2	1,873.49
R1	1,872.69
Previous close	1871.89
S1	1,871.09
S2	1,870.29
S3	1,869.49
S4	1,867.10
S5	1,864.30
S6	1,863.14

Open price

Long breakout trade.

B. Go short when price hits S4. Profit targets are S5 and S6. Stop loss is S3.

22-Apr	
R6	1,880.64
R5	1,879.48
R4	1,876.68
R3	1,874.29
R2	1,873.49
R1	1,872.69
Previous close	1871.89
S1	1,871.09
S2	1,870.29
S3	1,869.49 Stop loss
S4	1,867.10 Go short
S5	1,864.30 Profit
S6	1,863.14 targets

Open price (S3–S4)

Short breakout trade.

Testing the Camarilla Equation

Testing difficulties

Searching the Internet, one can easily find several people who claim to be successfully trading the Camarilla Equation, or to have had positive results using it. Of those, only a few of them supply some scarce anecdotal evidence and certainly not enough to assess the merits of any trading system.

The Camarilla Equation is supposed to work irrespective of the asset traded or the trade duration. It can therefore be used to trade stocks, indices, currencies, commodities and derivatives in any timeframe. This enormous variety of trading possibilities makes testing the Camarilla Equation a heavy duty task whose complexity is compounded if one wants to take into account the trading costs and spreads charged by different brokers. In addition some assets such as currency pairs are not traded in an exchange which means that the same trade may be executed at different prices depending on the broker who carries it out.

To test the Camarilla Equation for the markets, assets and timeframes that interests you I am therefore providing a tool that you can freely download from http://www.morbat.com/ntwz. It is an expert advisor that works with MetaTrader4 which is probably the most popular and ubiquitous trading platform today and made available by brokers worldwide.

Profit, loss and reward to risk

Since the Camarilla Equation provides precise entry and exit points for a trade we can calculate for each possible trade its maximum profit, its maximum loss and its limit reward to risk. With that information we can then calculate the minimum required win ratio for it to have a positive expectancy. Assuming that one exits the trade when the first profit level is reached, the calculations are as follows:

Reversal long trades

The **maximum profit per trade** is given by R1 - S3, or:

Maximum profit = (Close $_{N-1}$ + Range $_{N-1}$ x 1.1 / 12) - (Close $_{N-1}$ - Range $_{N-1}$ x 1.1 / 4)

Maximum profit = Range N-1 x 1.1 / 3

The **maximum loss per trade** is given by S3 - S4, or:

Maximum loss = (Close N-1 - Range N-1 x 1.1 / 4) - (Close N-1 - Range N-1 x 1.1 / 2)

Maximum loss = Range N-1 x 1.1 / 4

The limit reward to risk per trade is therefore:

Limit reward to risk = (Range N-1 x 1.1 / 3) / (Range N-1 x 1.1 / 4)

Limit reward to risk = 1.33(3).

Reversal short trades

The **maximum profit per trade** is given by R3 - S1, or:

Maximum profit = (Close N-1 + Range N-1 x 1.1 / 4) - (Close N-1 - Range N-1 x 1.1 / 12)

Maximum profit = Range N-1 x 1.1 / 3

Likewise, the **maximum loss per trade** is given by R4 - R3, or:

Maximum loss = (Close N-1 + Range N-1 x 1.1 / 2) - (Close N-1 + Range N-1 x 1.1 / 4)

Maximum loss = Range N-1 x 1.1 / 4

The limit reward to risk per trade is:

Limit reward to risk = (Range N-1 x 1.1 / 3) / (Range N-1 x 1.1 / 4)

Limit reward to risk = 1.33(3).

Breakout long trades

The **maximum profit per trade** is R5 - R4, or:

Maximum profit = (R4 + (R4 - R3) x 1.168) - (Close N-1 + Range N-1 x 1.1 / 2)

Maximum profit = Range N-1 x 1.1 / 4 x 1.168

Similarly, the **maximum loss per trade** is given by R4 - R3, or:

Maximum loss = (Close N-1 + Range N-1 x 1.1 / 2) - (Close N-1 + Range N-1 x 1.1 / 4)

Maximum loss = Range N-1 x 1.1 / 4

The limit reward to risk per trade is:

Limit reward to risk = (Range N-1 x 1.1 / 4 x 1.168) / (Range N-1 x 1.1 / 4)

Limit reward to risk = 1.168.

Breakout short trades

The **maximum profit per trade** is given by S4 - S5, or:

Maximum profit = S4 - (S4 - (S3 - S4) x 1.168)

Maximum profit = Range N-1 x 1.1 / 4 x 1.168

The **maximum loss per trade** is given by S3 - S4, or:

Maximum loss = (Close N-1 - Range N-1 x 1.1 / 4) - (Close N-1 - Range N-1 x 1.1 / 2)

Maximum loss = Range N-1 x 1.1 / 4

The limit reward to risk per trade is:

Limit reward to risk = (Range N-1 x 1.1 / 4 x 1.168) / (Range N-1 x 1.1 / 4)

Limit reward to risk = 1.168.

Required win ratio

The next table displays the minimum win ratio required to achieve a positive expectancy of 0.1 for each possible trade given its reward to risk.

Required Win Ratio	MEAN REVERSION	BREAKOUT
Win ratio	47.21%	50.74%
Reward to Risk	1.33	1.168
Expectancy	0.10	0.10

Remember, this is assuming that the trade is 100% exited on the first take profit level. You can define other exit rules, e.g. exiting 50% on the first take profit level and 50% on the second profit level, and then apply the same procedure to test for the asset and timeframe that interests you.

Again, to download the testing tool go to http://www.morbat.com/ntwz.

I wish you the all the best. Trade with common sense, have fun and make profits!

About the author

José Manuel Moreira Batista is a private trader and investor and manages private concerns. After graduating in Business Administration in 1982 he did a stint in the Air Force and then went on to hold executive positions in several multinational corporations until 1999.

That year he left the corporate world and started the management consulting and training company that he still owns today. He also taught university courses in Corporate Finance, Financial Accounting, Cost Accounting and Real Estate.

As an early display of his uncanny market timing he started trading the stock market in 1987. In case you are wondering, he did not lose money in the crash having been ~~lucky~~ savvy enough to exit all his positions a few days before Monday, October 19. He kept actively trading, studying and researching throughout the years.

His results-oriented books and courses blend experience with a sound theoretical foundation to deliver practical, easy-to-follow knowledge that brings immediate benefits to readers and students.

Disclaimer

The author and the publisher make no representations as to the accuracy, completeness, suitability or validity of any information in this book and will not be liable for any errors or omissions in this information or any damages arising from its display or use. The author and the publisher are neither providing investment advisory services nor acting as registered investment advisors or broker-dealers; they also do not purport to tell or suggest which securities or currencies anyone should buy or sell for themselves. The author and the publisher may hold positions in the stocks, currencies or industries discussed here. You understand and acknowledge that there is a very high degree of risk involved in trading and that the author and the publisher assume no responsibility or liability for your trading and investment results.

It should not be assumed that the methods, techniques, or indicators presented will be profitable or that they will not result in losses. Past results of any individual trader or trading system are not indicative of future returns by that trader or system, and are not indicative of future returns which may be realized by you. In addition, the indicators, strategies, writings, workbooks, spreadsheets, check lists; blueprints etc. are provided for informational and educational purposes only and should not be construed as investment or trading advice. You should not rely solely on the information provided in making any investment. Rather, you should use it only as a starting point for your own independent research in order to allow you to form your own opinion regarding trading and investments. In addition, you should always check with your licensed financial advisor and tax advisor to determine the suitability of any trading or investment.

HYPOTHETICAL OR SIMULATED PERFORMANCE RESULTS HAVE CERTAIN INHERENT LIMITATIONS. UNLIKE AN ACTUAL PERFORMANCE RECORD, SIMULATED RESULTS DO NOT REPRESENT ACTUAL TRADING AND MAY NOT BE IMPACTED BY BROKERAGE AND OTHER SLIPPAGE FEES. ALSO, SINCE THE TRADES HAVE NOT ACTUALLY BEEN EXECUTED, THE RESULTS MAY HAVE UNDER- OR OVER-COMPENSATED FOR THE IMPACT, IF ANY, OF CERTAIN MARKET FACTORS, SUCH AS LACK OF LIQUIDITY. SIMULATED TRADING PROGRAMS IN GENERAL ARE ALSO SUBJECT TO THE FACT THAT THEY ARE DESIGNED WITH THE BENEFIT OF HINDSIGHT. NO REPRESENTATION IS BEING MADE THAT ANY ACCOUNT WILL OR IS LIKELY TO ACHIEVE PROFITS OR LOSSES SIMILAR TO THOSE SHOWN.

The author or the publisher may have an affiliate relationship with all or some of the companies whose products or services are mentioned. This means that, at no additional cost to you, the author or the publisher may earn a commission or credit if you decide to buy any of their products or services.

www.ingramcontent.com/pod-product-compliance
Lightning Source LLC
Chambersburg PA
CBHW071819170526
45167CB00003B/1372